A LOOK AT NATURE'S CYCLES

CYCLES IN SPACE

BY BRAY JACOBSON

Gareth Stevens
PUBLISHING

CRASH COURSE

Please visit our website, www.garethstevens.com. For a free color catalog of all our high-quality books, call toll free 1-800-542-2595 or fax 1-877-542-2596.

Library of Congress Cataloging-in-Publication Data

Names: Jacobson, Bray, author.
Title: Cycles in space / Bray Jacobson.
Description: New York : Gareth Stevens Publishing, [2020] | Series: A look at nature's cycles | Includes bibliographical references and index.
Identifiers: LCCN 2018039578| ISBN 9781538241028 (pbk.) | ISBN 9781538241042 (library bound) | ISBN 9781538241035 (6 pack)
Subjects: LCSH: Astronomy--Juvenile literature. | Eclipses--Juvenile literature. | Seasons--Juvenile literature. | Moon--Phases--Juvenile literature. | Earth (Planet)--Orbit--Juvenile literature. | Solar system--Miscellanea--Juvenile literature.
Classification: LCC QB46 .J33 2019 | DDC 523.002--dc23
LC record available at https://lccn.loc.gov/2018039578

First Edition

Published in 2020 by
Gareth Stevens Publishing
111 East 14th Street, Suite 349
New York, NY 10003

Copyright © 2020 Gareth Stevens Publishing

Designer: Sarah Liddell
Editor: Kristen Nelson

Photo credits: Cover, p. 1 (main) vovan/Shutterstock.com; cover, p. 1 (inset) SW.ART/Shutterstock.com; arrow background used throughout Inka1/Shutterstock.com; p. 5 Vadim Sadovski/Shutterstock.com; p. 7 muratart/Shutterstock.com; p. 9 Jurik Peter/Shutterstock.com; p. 11 Vadim Petrakov/Shutterstock.com; pp. 13, 15, 19, 23 (background) guteksk7/Shutterstock.com; pp. 13 (diagram), 17 Designua/Shutterstock.com; p. 15 Studi8Neosiam/Shutterstock.com; p. 19 (diagram) Ramona Heim/Shutterstock.com; p. 21 sNike/Shutterstock.com; p. 23 (diagram) shooarts/Shutterstock.com; p. 25 Athapet Piruksa/Shutterstock.com; p. 27 sdecoret/Shutterstock.com; p. 29 Markus Gann/Shutterstock.com; p. 30 Castleski/Shutterstock.com.

Printed in the United States of America

CPSIA compliance information: Batch #CS19GS: For further information contact Gareth Stevens, New York, New York at 1-800-542-2595.

CONTENTS

Words in the glossary appear in **bold** type the first time they are used in the text.

INTO SPACE

What happens in space affects life on Earth! In fact, the seasons and how long night is are caused by the cycles of Earth's movement through space. The moon, sun, and stars all have cycles, too!

MAKE THE GRADE

A cycle is a set of steps or actions that happen over and over.
Sometimes, a part of a cycle is called a phase.

THE SOLAR CYCLE

It takes about 11 years for the sun to move through its solar cycle. Sunspots, or dark spots on the sun's surface, tell scientists a lot about what's happening during the solar cycle. These can become solar storms that send energy into space!

MAKE THE GRADE

Sunspots look dark when we look at pictures of the sun because they aren't as hot as the rest of the sun. They're still about 6,500°F (3,593°C) though!

The first part of the solar cycle is solar minimum. The

MAKE THE GRADE

At the end of the solar cycle, the **magnetic field** of the sun changes. This means the north and south poles of the sun switch places!

A lot of activity on the sun, like solar storms, can cause **auroras** in Earth's sky. It can also affect radio **communications** and electricity on Earth, as well as **satellites**. What happens in space truly does matter to our lives on Earth!

MAKE THE GRADE

Lots of solar activity can make it unsafe for astronauts to do their work in space!

AURORA

THE EARTH MOVES

Earth rotates, or spins. One complete rotation takes about 24 hours, or 1 day on Earth. When part of Earth faces the sun, it's day there. When part of Earth faces away from the sun, it's night there.

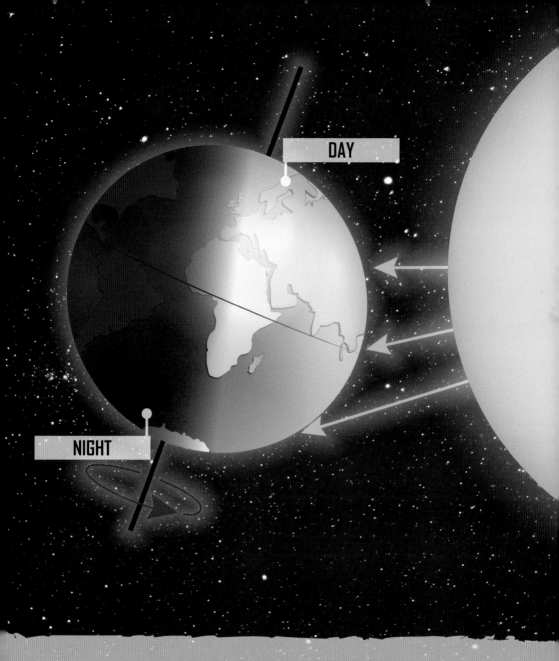

DAY

NIGHT

MAKE THE GRADE

Earth rotates on an axis, or the imaginary line around
which something spins.

Earth also moves around, or orbits, the sun. This is Earth's revolution. One revolution around the sun is a little bit longer than 365 days, or 1 year, on Earth. Earth's orbit looks like an ellipse, which is a circle that's been slightly flattened.

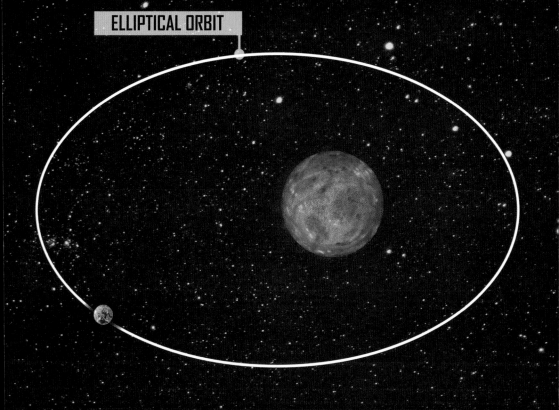

MAKE THE GRADE

During its orbit, Earth is not always the same distance
from the sun. It may be as far away as 94.5 million miles
(152 million km) or as close as 91 million miles (146 million km).

Earth's axis is **tilted** and always points in the same direction. So, as Earth revolves, different parts of Earth receive direct sunlight. Depending on the time of year, the North Pole or South Pole may be tilted toward the sun. This causes the seasons!

SEASONS IN THE NORTHERN **HEMISPHERE**

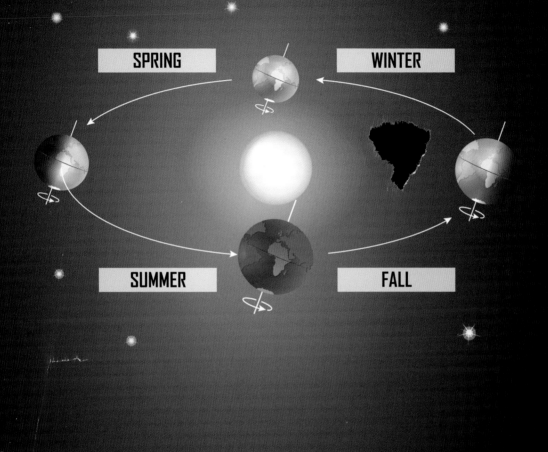

SPRING

WINTER

SUMMER

FALL

MAKE THE GRADE

Earth's tilt controls how high the sun can get in the sky in every place on Earth every day of the year.

The Northern and Southern Hemispheres don't have the same seasons at the same time. When it's winter in the Northern Hemisphere, it's summer in the Southern Hemisphere! This also has to do with Earth's tilt and revolution around the sun.

NORTHERN HEMISPHERE

EQUATOR

SOUTHERN HEMISPHERE

MAKE THE GRADE

The equator is the imaginary line that circles Earth, dividing the Northern and Southern Hemispheres. At the equator, the seasons don't change! It's always hot and the sun is high in the sky.

STAR CYCLES?

Earth's rotation and revolution create a cycle of stars in the sky, too. Stars appear to move during the night. They seem to rise in the east and set in the west. However, it's Earth's movement that makes them seem to move that way.

MAKE THE GRADE

Stars *do* move! All stars—the sun included—have orbits in our Milky Way **galaxy**. However, they're so far way, it takes us a long time to notice their movement.

As Earth orbits the sun over the course of a year, different constellations are **visible** to different parts of Earth. They seem to move west in the sky. In fact, you're just looking in a different direction into space during winter than summer!

MAKE THE GRADE

A constellation is a group of stars that seem to
form a picture or **pattern**. Over time, **astronomers** have
divided the sky into 88 constellations

THE LUNAR CYCLE

The moon appears to change shape in the sky. It doesn't! But the parts of the moon we can see change over the course of about a month. The moon's cycle, called the lunar cycle, is often divided into eight phases.

MAKE THE GRADE

The moon orbits Earth. It may seem to get bigger or smaller in the sky because its orbit is elliptical. The moon moves farther from and closer to Earth during this orbit.

No matter the time of the lunar cycle, we always see only one face, or side, of the moon. Sunlight **illuminates** the face of the moon. How much of the moon's face appears illuminated to us on Earth depends on the **angle** between the moon and the sun.

MAKE THE GRADE

No matter where you are on Earth, you'll see the same phase of the moon as everyone else!

When the moon is fully illuminated, it's called a full moon. When none of it is illuminated, it's called a new moon. Between these phases, the moon is only partly illuminated. Waning phases mean less of the moon is being illuminated. Waxing means more is being illuminated.

FULL MOON

NEW MOON

MAKE THE GRADE

The moon changes phase slowly. For example, the crescent
and gibbous phases last for about a week each!

PHASES OF THE MOON

FIRST QUARTER

WAXING GIBBOUS

WAXING CRESCENT

WAXING GIBBOUS

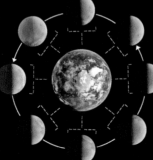

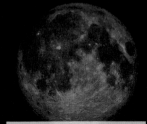

FULL

NEW

WANING GIBBOUS

WANING CRESCENT

THIRD QUARTER

GLOSSARY

angle: the space between two lines or surfaces at or close to the point where they meet

astronomer: a person who studies stars, planets, and other heavenly bodies

aurora: a happening in the sky in which streams of light appear because of extra energy in Earth's atmosphere, or the gases around the planet

communication: the ways of sending information to people using technology

galaxy: a large group of stars, planets, gas, and dust that form a unit within the universe

hemisphere: one-half of Earth

illuminate: to light up

magnetic field: the area around a magnet where its pull is felt. Earth has a magnetic field, too.

pattern: the way colors or shapes happen over and over again

satellite: an object that circles Earth in order to collect and send information or aid in communication

tilted: the state of having one side higher than the other

visible: able to be seen

FOR MORE INFORMATION

BOOKS

Ipcizade, Catherine. *Phases of the Moon*. North Mankato, MN: Pebble, 2018.

Mader, Jan. *How Do Planets Move?* New York, NY: Cavendish Square Publishing, 2019.

WEBSITES

The Phases of the Moon
www.natgeokids.com/au/discover/science/space/the-phases-of-the-moon/
Read even more about the lunar cycle here.

What Is an Orbit?
www.nasa.gov/audience/forstudents/5-8/features/nasa-knows/what-is-orbit-58.html
Learn more about orbits in space on this NASA website.

INDEX